MW00649168

HOW TO

MAKE
BEATS

Disclaimer:
There is no exact way of making a beat. This handbook
is intended to be a guideline on your beat-making journey.
This book is written in a way that encourages creativity. We
outline basic structure to beat making. The goal behind this
handbook is to help new producers understand and make
better beats.

The terms "beat maker" and "producer" are often used
interchangeably throughout this book.

If you run into any terminology you do not understand,
please reference our Music Production Terminology section
at the end of the handbook.

Copyright © 2020 Slime Green Beats

All rights reserved. No part of this book may be reproduced
or used in any manner without written permission of
the copyright owner except for the use of quotations in
a book review. For more information contact: support@
slimegreenbeats.com

First paperback edition

ISBN: 978-0-578-81785-9

CONTENTS

EQUIPMENT

This is some of the basic hardware and software needed to make beats. Be sure to reference the manual of the hardware/software you purchase in order to install the equipment correctly.*Prices below are liable to fluctuate.

1. **Keyboard** ($50–$150): Pick a keyboard based on your piano skill level. We suggest one where you can at least change the octaves. This is only needed if you plan on recording melodies and/or drums via a MIDI piano.

2. **Drum Pad** ($60–$200): For recording drums, having a drum pad can be a great addition. You can alternatively use a keyboard to record drums, although a separate drum pad is recommended. Some MIDI keyboards come with drum pads.

3. **Find a DAW (Digital Audio Workstation):** For example, FL Studio 20 Producer Edition is a great beginner DAW (Currently $199); however, we recommend buying the Signature Edition ($299), as it comes with more features. For more information, check out image-line.com/fl-studio/compare-editions.

4. **Headphones/Speakers** ($50–$1000+): We do not recommend trying to make beats with your stock computer speakers. You should try to find a good

pair of headphones or monitor speakers to make beats with. The price of this hardware can range from very basic headphones and speakers to much more expensive, professional-quality listening devices. We recommend you spend at least $50 starting off, and make it a goal to improve your equipment as you grow as a producer.

HOW TO MAKE BEATS

So how do you make a beat?

All you are doing is placing sounds in whatever order you choose to produce one cohesive chain of sounds.

This can be referred to as a beat, an instrumental, a song, a track, music, or a snippet (sample of a beat).

A beat can be played by itself or can be accompanied with vocals.

In this section we break down beat making into several key elements for you to understand and review.

Sound Selection

You need good sounds to make a good beat. Sound selection, simply put, is the sounds that you choose to make your music with.

Whatever sounds you choose are up to you: you should consider your genre, style, etc.

We suggest that you not only take your time picking sounds when making a beat, but we also suggest you take your time when searching for and downloading drum kits, sound presets, samples, and other types of sounds online.

There are plenty of free drum kits, sound presets, and samples you can download online. Just search, for example, "Free Drum Kits" on YouTube or Google.

If you're just starting off, download some free kits. Once you find your niche sound (R&B, hip-hop, trap, trap soul, EDM, etc.), you should then download or purchase more specific kits to cater to your sound.

There are other sounds you can search for and download, such as sample loops (which we cover in another section) or effects like a bird chirping or someone laughing; this can also include VST (Virtual Studio Technology) presets: sound presets for your VST (Electra2,for example).

The VSTs on your DAW come with presets; however, you can download or purchase more for enhanced quality/selection. These are known as "sound banks" or "sound presets."

Also note that certain sounds are simply popular right now; therefore, using new, popular kits can put you at an advantage. Again, however, the creativity of beat making and the sounds you choose are totally up to you.

Melody

This section is aimed specifically toward melodies as a whole and recording/creating melodies.

There are two ways to create a melody: you can place in notes, or you can play notes on a MIDI keyboard. We recommend playing your melodies. We say this because being able to play an instrument will carry beyond a DAW.

When recording a melody on a MIDI keyboard, we suggest hitting the record button before you have a pattern ready to go. Oftentimes you will play your best pattern first. Beats are not meant to be overcomplicated; what you come up with first or second, more times than not, will work.

You can always edit your recording or note placement as many times as you like. This is a major benefit of using a DAW.

When selecting sounds for a melody (just like every other part of the process), you want to pick high-quality sounds. This means that in order to create the best melodies, you need to have the best VSTs with the best sounds.

You want sounds that mesh well. You want your patterns to not be too repetitive. If your melody is too repetitive, switch the melody up by adding new sounds, filters, or whatever makes it interesting.

Don't hesitate to layer sounds, especially chords. This will create a fuller, more unique sound. This does not always work like magic, but you should give it a try.

Samples

If you decide to include samples into your beat, you need to understand that there are two types of samples: royalty and royalty-free. If you are a beginner, we suggest focusing on royalty-free samples. "Royalty-free" means you do not have to pay anyone if the track makes money.

Sites like Looperman have royalty-free samples, so you can use them for free.

You must learn the DAW system so you can manipulate the sample. Once you get that done, you figure out the bpm (beats per minute) of the sample, and then you layer the snares, kicks, hi-hats, etc. on the sample.

Again, we suggest checking out Looperman to grab easy-to-go, free melody loops. There are also tons of free and paid loops included in drum kits and sample packs that you can download online.

Drums

This section is dedicated to the most commonly used drum sounds when making a beat. Drums set the mood of the track; drums give life to the beat. Drums are a feel.

There is an infinite number of drums, so this topic is very diverse by nature.

Our advice is to listen to the genre of music you want your drums to sound like. If you like reggaeton drums, listen to reggaeton music.

Once you get a feel for the sound, get drum kits based on the sound you want.

Once you get the kits, add your own flair to them.

Always tap the drum rhythm by hand. The drums should flow through your body.

Hi-Hats

Hi-hats set the pace of a beat. They can be used to emphasize the more up-tempo parts in a song. They can also be used to slow things down.

The sound of hi-hats, of all of these sounds, is the hardest to describe.

The key to using hi-hats is to make them flow with your beat.

Different genres of music have different popular hi-hat styles. Trap beat hi-hats, for example, tend to be more erratic and choppy. R&B hi-hats and underground hip-hop hi-hats tend to be more smooth and steady.

Let the hi-hats control the pace of the beat; imagine an artist laying vocals over your hi-hats if you ever get confused.

Open Hi-Hats

This is not to be confused with regular hi-hats. An open hi-hat is what it sounds like: more open and with a longer sound.

If we had to sound it out, it would sound like "tsssssss." You hear this sound a lot in classic hip-hop and R&B beats.

Open hi-hats will not always be usable in beat. You have to see if they are a good fit; don't force this sound into the beat if it does not sound right. However, if used properly, it can add more bounce to your drums.

What an open hi-hat typically does is connect the kick/808 and the snare/clap.

Next time you are listening to hip-hop or R&B music, pay attention to how the open hi-hat is used.

Kicks

The kick is the bounce to the beat. The name "kick" is a great name for it because it perfectly describes its usage.

When a beat is stale, the kick is what takes it up a notch (as with the 808). Therefore, the kick is best used during more upbeat parts of a song.

You can do a lot with the kick to shape the sound to how you want it:

- ❯ You can increase the velocity (although this should only be used for emphasis).
- ❯ You can increase the volume of the kick.
- ❯ You can stack the kick with another kick.
- ❯ You can use a VST effect to add distortion of emphasis.

Whatever you do, make sure you add some type of tool to prevent it from clipping in the final mix.

*To do all of these things above, we suggest watching videos on how producers modify kicks and see what works best for you.

The most important detail in the kick sound is picking a kick from the right drum kit that fits your beat the best.

As far as patterns go, take your time and create something that flows with the beat.

When making the beat, we recommend adding the kick after adding the hi-hats.

Snare

The snare marks the consistency and the tempo of a beat. It's that crack in the beat that keeps the time for the musician.

A rapper knows how to pace their rhymes based on the snare. It is very important to have this element in every beat.

A great snare is essential to getting the sound you want out of a track; you want it to hit as perfectly as possible.

A strong, crispy snare can also bring out the lower-end drum kicks/808 bass in the track and make them jump out even more.

Pay attention to these snare/drum layers, as you want the drum kick and snare to play off of each other to really make a memorable track.

As far as effects go, you can add reverb to the snare. This is a very common technique in music production to give a layer of depth to the mix. This will make the snare sound wider.

Ultimately, the most important thing with a snare is sound selection.

The snare is one sound that NEEDS to be consistent throughout a beat; therefore, picking the right sound is even more important because you will hear that sound hit over and over again.

You can add style to it, but it needs to be in tempo so an artist can expect its arrival and synchronize the snare with their vocals.

808 Versus Bass

If you're a chef in the kitchen, the 808 and bass are the spice. The specific sound they provide is an essential ingredient to making the food taste good; without it, the food will be bland.

The 808 sound is created from a DAW, while the bass sound comes from a low-end instrument like a bass drum or bass guitar.

While 808s and basslines are two different "sounds," they are used very similarly in a beat. Both are low-end sounds. For example, imagine a musician playing a bass drum. The musician can achieve a loud and low-end rumble. You can also produce a low-end bass rumble with an instrument like a bass guitar. The key difference between the low-end "sounds" is in the instrument used, release/sustain, punchiness of the sound (attack), octave, etc.

Key terms for this section:

- ❯ Attack - The impact/"punchiness" of the sound.
- ❯ Dryer sound - A computerized sound, lacking expression. Less release/sustain.
- ❯ Release/sustain - The sound duration.
- ❯ Wetter sound - Has more expression. More release/sustain.

808s

808s can sometimes sound very similar to the kick. Compared to basslines, they have a stronger attack with a shorter release/sustain.

The 808 is a dryer sound. It gives a thump to the beat.

Wetness and dryness can determine the mood of an 808.

Wetter 808s work better with slower and smoother beats. Dryer 808s work better with aggressive or up-tempo beats.

For a cohesive sound, it is best for the 808 to have a similar pattern to that of the melody. However, you don't have to use as many notes as the melody because the 808 acts like a tuned bass drum.

The more 808s you use, the more aggressive the beat will be. Fewer 808s can add more of a "bouncy" sound similar to the sound you would hear in the south, in particular Louisiana.

As far as mixing effects go, distortion is a very common effect to use with 808s. However, you don't have to distort every 808; it just depends on your style.

Bass

A bassline is more musical and wetter in sound. Compared to an 808, it has a weaker attack with a longer release/sustain.

As far as effects go, like with 808s, try adding distortion to your basslines for that extra razzle-dazzle.

If you struggle with basslines, don't be overwhelmed, just understand that it is a low-end melody. Typically, the bassline follows the melody already established. Treat the bass like a complement to the melody.

We do not like to touch too much on the creative process, but if you struggle with adding good bass or 808 patterns, add this sound right after you add the melody. Don't wait until the end of your beat-making process to add the bass or 808.

Note: you can use an 808 and bassline separately or at the same time. If used at the same time, they have to be at different frequencies. If you're a beginner, we suggest trying one sound at a time. We understand this section is a bit advanced; however, we felt it was necessary for beginners to understand how low-end sounds work in beats.

Mixing

This section is more advanced, and we are going to dive right into the technical side of things. We understand as a beginner you may have a hard time grasping these concepts. Use this handbook as a reference guide for when you are ready to implement the following.

So what is mixing?

Mixing is maximizing the potential of every sound in your track.

When mixing, the gain level for a sound is important. The gain level is the volume of a sound. Too much volume equals too much compression.

Make sure you don't have too much gain so you don't over compress your track. You want the cleanest sound possible.

You want the gain level to be neither too loud nor too quiet.

You want the sound to be as vibrant as possible. You can use VSTs, like Ozone, to find the right mix.

With mixing, you should use plug-ins to take the high ends and low ends out. This is how you customize sounds and start being creative.

The "high ends" are sounds on the higher end of the sound spectrum, such as hi-hats, vocals, and snares. The "low ends" are deeper sounds, such as bass, 808s, and kicks.

Remember: there is no set way to mix(there are fundamentals, like not overcompressing and don't clip), but you want your sound to be as clean as possible. Use your ears and be creative.

Arrangement

When it comes to arrangement, we break it down into a simple method. There are tons of videos and songs with different styles of arrangement. The arrangement of your beat should be tailored to the type of music you are making.

That being said, here are our simple rules for arrangement:

1. Arrangement is like a basketball: imagine dribbling it with one hand, then switching it to the other hand. That is how a beat should flow. A beat should never be boring. There can be similar parts, but in general, the entire beat needs to have different parts all throughout. However, you will need to balance this out with repetitive elements. There is a yin and yang balance. One way to get better at arrangement is by listening to your favorite songs and noting down the patterns on a piece of paper.

2. As noted above, you want to keep switching a beat up. We recommend every four bars; there needs to be a different element to keep the listener interested.

3. The changes can be as simple as switching up the melody, having a different drum pattern, or using some kind of filter. Note: you can also take sounds away to switch up the melody; it is not always adding, it is also subtracting.

WHAT MAKES
A GREAT
PRODUCER?

If we could sum up how to become great at beatmaking in one sentence, it would be this: make beats a lifestyle, watch tutorials, and get feedback.

The Lifestyle

Shape your life around making beats. Everything you do should be a conscious effort towards making higher-quality beats.

Know what you have to do *in your life* to make the best beats that *you* can make.

- ❯ If you focus better, and therefore make better beats, during a certain time of the day, try to make beats during that time.

- ❯ Do you need to eat or drink while creating? Maybe coffee helps you focus better. Whatever works for you.

- ❯ Do you make better beats when no one is around, or do you prefer to collaborate?

There are tons of little nuances that make you feel more comfortable and allow you to be in your *zone*.

An easy thing you can do when making a beat is put your phone away. This will help you focus much better.

Avoid people that negatively criticize you making beats or the quality of your beats. Get rid of all negative objects or associations in your area while you make beats.

Consider cleaning up your beat-making area or studio (whether that be at home or abroad). An uncluttered environment equals an uncluttered mind.

Surround yourself with positive and relaxing imagery. Make yourself as comfortable, relaxed, and happy as possible when you make beats.

If you ever find yourself making uninspiring beats, or experiencing what's known as "beat block," simply take a break for a couple of days, then come back.

Watch Tutorials

Tutorials will give you ideas and knowledge on how to use your DAW to make better beats.

The key is to watch tutorials in a way that does not suppress creativity. Watch tutorials on specific subjects such as kicks, snares, tools, mixing, or arrangement. Try not to watch too many tutorials where someone makes a beat a certain way: it will make you feel as though you have to make a beat that exact way to be successful.

A safe alternative is listening to popular music. Focus on both your genre and music outside your genre. This can give you a great idea of structure as well as creative ideas for your music.

Avoid watching tutorials (or getting feedback) from artists that aren't making great beats. I know it seems obvious, but learning from people that aren't much better than you may only confuse the process.

Get Feedback

Getting feedback on a beat is a surprisingly easy thing to do, but most producers don't want to do this.

Let me tell you, though, feedback can help you improve much faster.

Make beats, get feedback, and implement feedback. It is a simple formula for success.

Easy places to get feedback online: forums and Reddit.

You can get feedback off-line as well. Remember, get feedback from beat makers that are better than you or know subjects within beatmaking much better than you.

Feedback can be extremely helpful in guiding you towards a more comprehensive beat. Once you start getting less and less negative feedback and more positive feedback, that is a sign that your beatmaking is getting much better.

However, as they say, success can be a bad teacher: that means that people telling you your beats are awesome all the time doesn't help. It makes you feel better about your work, but it won't help you improve. That being said, have thick skin and don't be afraid to constantly ask for feedback.

22

ONLINE MARKETING

It is not a secret that the internet has expanded the reach and possibilities of digital products such as beats. Knowing a bit about internet marketing can help you gain exposure as a music producer.

We broke this section down into a couple of sites that we have personally used and have had success with marketing beats online. As this book ages, there will be more websites to market your music on. As a recommendation, you need to be conscious of what is trending in the industry. There will always be some form of technology/social media that people gravitate toward.

YouTube

YouTube is a very popular online video-sharing website. To have success there you need to create good graphics/videos and upload your best beats.

For more views, you can name them "type beats" (beats that are like major artists or genres), for instance, "Eminem type beat" or "R&B flute beat." This will get more views simply because these are terms that are being searched for at a higher volume.

If you ever have trouble finding good keywords to use, try a site like keywordtool.io/youtube.

Keep this simple formula: good beats + good graphics = more views. Constantly work on improving both of these, and you will get better results (more views on your beats).

Instagram

Many serious artists are on Instagram. It has become a must in the music industry.

Take your Instagram profile seriously. Don't make it too spammy. Instead, promote it and nurture it.

Instagram is a great place to network and meet new artists. Instagram is also a great place to connect with artists that found you on other sites, like YouTube.

Take cool photos of your work, maybe snippets of your beats, and upload them.

Develop an online personality and establish your brand: you never know who's looking.

Future Producers/IllMuzik

Both Future Producers (futureproducers.com) and IllMuzik (illmuzik.com) are popular music production forums.

On these sites you can find just about anything producer related.

You can get great feedback on your work from a truly constructive environment. There are a lot of successful producers on there that post regularly. You can mingle and learn a lot from them in a comfortable environment.

SoundCloud

SoundCloud makes it very easy to upload music, and it has enough popularity to make your time there worthwhile.

We suggest you build your SoundCloud account in a similar way you would with YouTube. The major difference is that with SoundCloud you do not need to create videos.

We have had good success on SoundCloud; we believe it is worth using.

Email Marketing

Now, here's a secret to selling beats online and getting placements (getting your beats used by artists): you don't need a website to have success, just email your contacts. One of the great advantages of beats is that they are a digital product and can be sent to artists completely over the internet.

Email marketing, or sending your beats and building relationships with clients via email, works great.

Here's another tip: when you upload your beats to YouTube or SoundCloud, be sure to include your email with every beat so artists know how to contact you.

Understand that you need to build relationships with artists before they will use your beats or buy your beats.

We can tell you from experience that one artist or manager can make you $200/month or more. You don't need hundreds of random followers or a sophisticated internet marketing funnel to make money in this industry.

You just need to collect emails, send great beats, and listen and respond to the artists you are working with.

Not sure how to get emails? Here's a neat trick: ask and search. That's right, just find rappers and ask for their emails.

A lot of the time, the artist's email will be in their Twitter or Instagram bio. Also, try searching "send beats" on Twitter and check out the tweets. You can find some great emails just by searching for that phrase. Be sure to introduce yourself, send your best work every time, and don't spam.

THE ULTIMATE GUIDE TO BEAT LICENSING

If you want to sell beats to artists, it is important to understand beat licensing.

There are two types of beats typically sold in this industry: lease beats and exclusive beats (also referred to as "nonexclusive" and "exclusive" beats).

Lease Beats vs. Exclusive Beats

First, you need to know the meaning of these two licenses.

With lease beats, the producer has the right to lease the beat multiple times to different customers.

With exclusive beats, the producer can only sell the beat once to one artist. The artist that purchases the beat has exclusive rights to its usage.

Lease beats are less expensive and can be sold more; however, they often do not include royalties. When the lease, or usage limit, of the beat is reached, the customer has to purchase the lease again. These types of beats are more often sold to beginner and intermediate artists.

Exclusive beats are more expensive but can only be sold once. They often include royalties. They do not have a usage limit.

Be sure to discuss, understand, and be clear on the terms of your beat when distributing.

Let's expand on the advantages and disadvantages of these two licenses so you can get a more concrete understanding.

Advantages of Lease Beats

1. **Multiple Selling:** A single track can be sold a few times to several customers. If you are a music producer, you will have the opportunity to sell the beat again and again.

2. **Cheap in Price:** As the producer sells a single beat repeatedly to customers, the lease beats are cheaper and more affordable for newcomer musicians. It is easier to persuade an amateur artist to purchase a beat for $20–$50 versus $150–$2000+ (the typical pricing of lease versus exclusive beats).

3. **Healthy Market:** There is a good market of rappers looking to lease beats. For an up-and-coming rapper, they can get some pretty dope beats for an affordable price from a producer. It's

a great way to capitalize on the growing number of up-and-coming rappers. Lease beats are more popular online than exclusive beats.

Disadvantages of Lease Beats

1. **Low price:** You will not make as much money from selling a lease beat. You are sacrificing the ability to sell it as an exclusive for whatever amount of money you accept for the lease. (You cannot sell a leased beat as an exclusive to another artist.)

2. **Distribution Limit:** If you lease a beat, after a certain number of distributions, you have to re-lease the beat. That means that you will have to contact the artist yourself or hope they uphold the lease limit (if you set one).

Advantages of Selling Exclusive Beats

1. **Up-Front Money:** The producer can earn more with a single selling. There is no chance of selling the same beat twice. The up-front money is quite assured and often considered profitable.

2. **Professional:** Exclusive beats are professional, and the price of every beat justifies the seriousness or skill level of the vocal artist.

3. **The Format of the Beat:** The artist will often request track outs, which are splits of each mixer

channel. To do this on your DAW, search "how to track out in (your DAW)." This allows the artist to do whatever they want with the beats.

4. **Royalties:** The scope of earning money does not close after selling the exclusive beats for the first time. A producer can make a deal regarding future royalties on the published music. This is quite fascinating for the musician too. A liaison between the seller and musical artist will bring reputation for both of them.

The most disadvantageous side of exclusive beats is the price. The price is sometimes too high for a newcomer or an artist on a tight budget to afford. It can be much harder to find clients that want to purchase exclusive beats. The quality of the beat you make also has to be much higher to get these types of sales. It took about three years of practice for us to sell an exclusive beat for more than $200; whereas, we were able to sell lease beats year one.

Our Recommendation

For newcomers, it is best to start with lease beats. You are more likely to sell there when starting off.

After having a good reputation in the industry, the producer may start selling exclusive beats.

If you are interested in understanding the quality needed to sell an exclusive beat, just search for "sold beats" on YouTube.

Above all, remember that the quality of your beats is important, but the relationships you build with artists are equally if not more valuable to your success.

Don't worry too much about sales, the primary focus should be on improving your craft.

CONCLUSION

This handbook should cover all the basics of beat making. To follow up, we recommend you subscribe to our channel: YouTube.com/SlimeGreenBeats.

We have plenty of videos and resources to further your beat-making career. You can also message us at any time if you have any questions along the way!

We very much appreciate you purchasing this handbook. We understand that beats are a creative subject, and we did our very best to present our knowledge in words without limiting creativity.

We hope you can succeed in the music industry as we have. We promise it is possible; we too started from nothing.

-Slime Green Beats

Contact

Email: contact@slimegreenbeats.com

YouTube: YouTube.com/SlimeGreenBeats

MUSIC PRODUCTION TERMINOLOGY

The following are common production terms used in the rap/hip-hop music industry. This list is compiled and written by Slime Green Beats. Definitions are based on knowledge and experience in the industry.

Analogue – Type of wave signal that is continuous.

Automation – Process where the software will remember user inputs, like pitch modulation, note velocity, etc.

Bass – The low filter noise, typically on a lower octave or as a deeper sound. Used as the background in a lot of beats. Almost every good beat has this.

Beat – A musical composition created by a music producer, typically for the use of an artist to record vocals over.

Bit Depth – Number of bits in a sample (computer engineering term for storing data).

Bounce or Bouncing – What makes your head move up and down, inexplicable like the juice, sauce, etc.

BPM – The beats per minute of a musical recording or sample. This is essentially the metronome of the beat.

Channel — Where a specific instrument is playing from in a mix, usually denoted by a number.

Chords — A set of notes played at the same time.

Chorus — Part of a track that sounds more epic than the rest. Typically louder and leads the sound or beat. Producers can often struggle with this sound, making it too loud at times, or not loud enough, and either of those make a weird mix.

Clipping — Any distortion or sound you don't want in a mix due to overloading software.

Compression — Reducing the size of an audio signal to produce less or more sound.

Compressor — Lets you adjust gain, ratios, etc. Each one is unique.

Decibel — A way to measure sound level on a log scale (you'll learn in school that it's exponential).

Digital Audio Workstation (DAW) — An application typically run from a computer that acts as a digital orchestra. These applications are made to make music. They can be done on a computer and can often produce an array of sounds difficult to find in instrument form.

Dry — A reverberation effect that gives less perceived depth.

Drum Kit — Producers often create sounds to sell or give away. These drum kits often include snares, hi-hats, kicks, 808s, percussion, and FX.

Emcee or MC — In traditional hip-hop, it stands for "Master or Ceremonies." Basically it's a rapper that performs well on stage.

Equalization (EQ) — A device that lets you tweak the

sounds within an audio clip. This is often a solution to specific volume issues.

Exclusive — A beat only sold to one individual. Typically, if not always, at a higher price than a lease. The producer cannot legally resell the same beat to another artist.

Folder — A place where files can be placed and obtained on a DAW application. Often in the browser setting.

FX — "Effect" for a sound.

Gain — Increase ratio of a variable to another.

High Pass Filter — Passes signals with frequency higher than cutoff frequency.

High Range Filter — Filters out the high frequency tones of a beat.

Hip-Hop — A musical genre started by African Americans. It has since become quite popular and has reached out to many subgenres, including trap, rap, R&B, and underground.

Hook — Part of a beat, usually with words that the artist uses to shape the song with. After a rapper or singer goes through their first verse, the hook will play, which leads into the second and third verse. The hook appears two to three times throughout the song and is the same each time.

Hz — Unit of frequency.

Impedance — Resistance in an audio device (measured in ohms).

Instrumental — Another word/synonym for "beat." A composition created by a musician usually to be sold to an artist or any buyer for commercial use.

Latency — Delay/lag.

Lease/Non-exclusive – A type of beat that the producer can legally sell to multiple artists. The price is typically, if not always, cheaper than an exclusive beat. The term "lease" implies that after a certain number of uses, the buyer has to re-lease the beat. Number of uses depends on which producer you lease from.

Loudness – The frequency of sound achieved through compression and volume adjustments.

Low Pass Filter – Passes signals with frequency lower than cutoff frequency.

Low Range Filter – Filters out the low frequency tones of a beat.

Master/Mastering Audio – Final element of making a track that involves getting the right levels, effects, etc. for a mix. Using digital sound techniques to produce higher quality sounding audio. Using things such as plugins, equalizers, and volume knobs on specific instruments. A number of things can be done, as this is a big phase and a part of producing a beat.

Metronome – Keeps beats/time at intervals.

MIDI – Musical instrument for recording/playing music electronically. Typically a device plugged into a computer that connects to the DAW(digital audio workstation). This device can be a keyboard, drum pad, tuner, or some other audio device. Users can manage the DAW application from the MIDI device.

Mid Range Filter – Filters out the mid-frequency tones (in between lows and highs) of a beat.

Mixer – Where you adjust sound levels, add effects, etc.

MP3 – A type of audio file extension.

Music Theory – The study of music.

Ohm – A unit measure of resistance.

Panning – In mix, where you hear the main sound coming out of the stereo.

Piano Roll Editor – Where a producer or engineer edits the individual notes in a pattern.

Plug-Ins – Applications within a DAW that create and modify sounds.

Quantization – Chopping/breaking down notes into smaller sections.

Rapper – Adds verbiage or "raps" to a beat. Typically dealt the task of performing in front of an audience. Rappers may "freestyle," write, or recitelyrics. Today's rappers can't do much in the modern industry without good producers on staff. However, in return, the live performances have gotten better.

Rap – A term often used interchangeably with "hip-hop," an urban type music genre known for its often raw, uncut, and creative nature.

Render – The processing of a sound or playlist. Typically referring to the exporting process of a track and how long it takes to create a file (MP3, WAVE, FLAC, etc.).

Resistance – Property relating to the passage of current.

Reverb – Similar to an echo in terms of a sound modification.

Samples/Sampling – The reuse of a sound recording recorded at a separate time.Producers use these samples in a DAW to formulate a beat around. This is typically a final step for producers, as it costs money to clear/ use samples. In terms of time length, samples only last a couple bars or less than thirty seconds.

Sample Libraries – A pack of samples. Clearance/legality is debatable. Samples can come in packs of up to 100 or more.

Sound Presets – You can often find sound presets for synth VSTs online. These are extra sounds, such as a piano or pad, that you can add to your synth preset library.

Synth – Generated signals that are converted to sounds through audio devices.

Synthesizer (Synth) – A harmonic sound application or instrument that produces an array of sounds that can be coordinated with piano or drum usage. Often used by producers to get a unique array of sounds.

Tap Tempo – A program in FL Studio that estimates the tempo based on real time tapping in the DAW.

Tempo – Rate music moves at.

Velocity – The speed a key is hit, used for emphasis on a sound.

Virtual Studio Technology (VST) – Software interface that lets users use effects, editors, etc.

WAVE – A type of file extension that carries the most data. Ideal for highest quality of audio production.

Waveform – The sound waves associated with a sound-based file. The waves illustrate the frequency/gain of an individual sound in a track. This is often used to master tracks and make sure everything's close to the same wavelength.

Wet – A reverberation effect that gives more perceived depth.

LINKS/
REFERENCES

Here are links to the websites mentioned in this handbook:

FL Studio: https://www.image-line.com/fl-studio-download/

Future Producers: https://www.futureproducers.com/forums/

IllMuzik: https://www.illmuzik.com/

Instagram: https://www.instagram.com/

Looperman: https://www.looperman.com/

SoundCloud: https://soundcloud.com/

YouTube: https://www.youtube.com/slimegreenbeats

RECOMMENDED SYNTH VSTS

We suggest the following synth VSTs to create melodies, effects, and basslines:

Electra2: https://www.tone2.com/electra2.html (mentioned in handbook)

Omnisphere: https://support.spectrasonics.net/manual/ Omnisphere2/25/en/topic/get-started-installation-page01b

Nexus: https://refx.com/nexus/

Sakura: https://www.image-line.com/plugins/Synths/ Sakura/

SynthMaster Player: https://www.kv331audio.com/ synthmasterplayer.aspx

Helm: https://tytel.org/helm/

Dexed: https://asb2m10.github.io/dexed/

Tunefish4: https://www.tunefish-synth.com/index.php/ download

Made in the USA
Columbia, SC
15 April 2024

34424409R00024